Dad JOKES

*201 terribly good
puns, one-liners and riddles
to make Your Family eye-roll and groan*

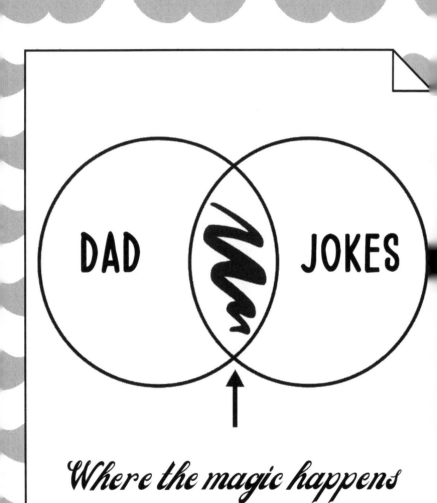

WHY ARE MOUNTAINS SO FUNNY?

BECAUSE THEY'RE
HILL-ARIOUS

HOW DO TREES GET ONLINE?

THEY JUST LOG-IN

IF YOU GO TO SLEEP WITH AN ITCHY BUM,

YOU WAKE UP WITH A SMELLY FINGER

HOW DOES A MAN ON THE MOON CUT HIS HAIR?

HE ECLIPSED IT.

MY SON ASKED ME IF I HAD SEEN THE DOG BOWL.

I SAID NO, I DIDN'T EVEN KNOW IT COULD DO THAT.

AIR IS NO LONGER FREE AT THE GAS STATION; NOW, IT'S $2.00. CAN I TELL YOU WHY?

INFLATION.

YOU SHOULD NOT IRON YOUR FOUR-LEAF CLOVER, YOU KNOW WHY?

BECAUSE YOU SHOULDN'T PRESS YOUR LUCK.

WHAT'S A HIKER'S FAVORITE DRINK?

MOUNTAIN DEW.

WHY DOES YOUR DOG KEEP BARKING AT THE SIGHT OF FOOD?

THAT'S WHAT I GET FOR BUYING A PURE BREAD DOG.

SOMEONE TOLD ME MY DAD WAS STEALING FROM HIS JOB AS A TRAFFIC COP,
I DIDN'T BELIEVE THIS, BUT ALL THE SIGNS WERE THERE WHEN HE GOT HOME.

MY DAD SPENT A LOT OF TIME, MONEY, AND EFFORT CHILDPROOFING MY HOUSE...

BUT THE KIDS STILL GET IN.

I SHOULD NEVER HAVE BELIEVED MY MOTHER WHEN I WAS A KID; SHE TOLD ME I COULD BE ANYONE I WANTED TO BE.

IT TURNS OUT THAT IDENTITY THEFT IS A CRIME.

WHAT DO SPRINTERS EAT BEFORE A RACE?

NOTHING, THEY FAST!

A GUY HAS A MEDICAL CONDITION; HE DOESN'T KNOW IF IT IS PSYCHOLOGICAL OR NOT. HE GOES TO HIS DOCTOR AND SAYS, "DOCTOR, I HAVE A CONDITION; I CAN SEE TOO MUCH INTO THE FUTURE." THE DOCTOR ASKS HIM, "HOW LONG HAVE YOU SUFFERED FROM THAT CONDITION?"

THE GUY TELLS HIM, "SINCE NEXT MONDAY."

MY WIFE COMPLAINS THAT I DON'T BUY HER CHOCOLATES. TO BE HONEST, I DIDN'T KNOW SHE SOLD CHOCOLATES.

DO YOU KNOW WHAT HAPPENS WHEN YOU MISTAKENLY PUT YOUR HAND IN A BLENDER? YOU GET A HANDSHAKE.

WHY COULDN'T THE BICYCLE
STAND UP BY ITSELF?

IT WAS TWO TIRED!

HAVE YOU BEEN TO THE
RESTAURANT ON THE MOON?
WHAT WAS IT LIKE?

GREAT FOOD, NO ATMOSPHERE!

WHAT'S THE DIFFERENCE BETWEEN A MAN DRESSED IN SHORTS ON A TRICYCLE AND A WELL-DRESSED MAN ON A BICYCLE?

ATTIRE!

WHY DID THE BEE'S HAIR STICK TO MY PALM?

BECAUSE BEES USE A HONEYCOMB.

WHY DO DADS TAKE AN EXTRA PAIR OF SOCKS WHEN THEY GO GOLFING?

IN CASE THEY GET
A HOLE IN ONE.

MY TOOTH ACHES; I NEED TO GO
TO THE DENTIST.
WHAT TIME IS IT?

TOOTH-HURTY.

WHY AREN'T KOALAS REGARDED AS REAL BEARS? BECAUSE THEY DON'T MEET THE KOALAFICATIONS.

I WENT FOR AN INTERVIEW FOR A JOB TODAY. THE MANAGER TOLD ME THEY NEEDED SOMEONE RESPONSIBLE. I REPLIED THAT I WAS RESPONSIBLE. "IN MY LAST JOB, THEY ALWAYS SAY I'M RESPONSIBLE WHEN ANYTHING HAPPENS.

WHY DO DOGS FLOAT IN WATER?

BECAUSE THEY ARE
GOOD BUOYS.

MUM GOT ME A SHOE MADE OF
A BANANA,

AND IT IS CALLED A SLIPPER!

AT A JOB INTERVIEW, I WAS OFFERED WATER. SO I FILLED IT TO THE BRIM AND EVEN ALLOWED IT TO OVERFLOW A BIT. THE INTERVIEWER ASKED ME, "NERVOUS?" I TOLD HIM NO, I ALWAYS GIVE OVER 100%

MY WIFE LEFT A NOTE IN THE FRIDGE SAYING, "THIS IS NOT WORKING; I'M GOING TO MY MOTHER'S HOUSE." I OPENED THE FRIDGE AND SAW THE LIGHTS ON, AND THE JUICE WAS COLD; EVERYTHING INSIDE WAS COLD. I'M CONFUSED; WHAT DID SHE MEAN?

WHICH IS THE MOST INTERESTING
BUILDING IN THE WORLD?

THE LIBRARY - IT'S GOT THE
MOST STORIES.

DO YOU KNOW THAT THIS BEEHIVE
HAS NO EXIT?

IT IS UNBEE-LIEVABLE.

I GAVE MY DAD HIS 50TH BIRTHDAY CARD. HE LOOKED AT ME AND SAID:

"YOU KNOW, ONE WOULD HAVE BEEN ENOUGH."

DAD JOKES ARE SO COOL.

SOMETIMES HE LAUGHS.

THE SCARECROW WAS GIVEN AN
AWARD BECAUSE HE WAS
OUT-STANDING IN HIS FIELD!

THIS GRAVEYARD LOOKS
OVERCROWDED.

YET PEOPLE ARE DYING
TO GET IN THERE!

THE GUY WHO STOLE MY DIARY
DIED YESTERDAY.

MY THOUGHTS ARE WITH HIS
FAMILY; THEY CAN KEEP IT.

THERE'S THIS FRUIT, IT IS
ORANGE IN COLOR, BUT IT
SOUNDS LIKE A PARROT?

A CARROT!

DO YOU KNOW WHY VAMPIRES HAVE
NO FRIENDS?

BECAUSE THEY SUCK!

I JUST SAW A NINJA! HE WAS
WEARING HIS FAVORITE SHOE...

SNEAKERS!

I JUST SAW THE COACH YELLING AT A VENDING MACHINE; WHY?

HE WANTED HIS QUARTER BACK.

VAMPIRES HARDLY FALL SICK, BUT WHEN THEY DO, THEY'RE ALWAYS

COFFIN.

WHAT DID THE GRAPE DO WHEN HE WAS STEPPED ON?

HE GAVE WINE

DAD, DID YOU GET A HAIR CUT?

NO, I CUT ALL OF IT.

IF TOWELS COULD TELL JOKES,
I THINK THEY'D HAVE A VERY DRY
SENSE OF HUMOR.

I WAS SO TIRED THAT I SLEPT
LIKE A LOG OF WOOD LAST
NIGHT. GUESS WHERE I WOKE
UP....

IN THE FIREPLACE!

WHAT DO YOU CALL A FISH
WEARING A BOWTIE?

SOFISHTICATED.

I USED TO RUN A DATING
SERVICE FOR CHICKENS.

BUT I WAS STRUGGLING TO
MAKE HENS MEET.

I KNOW A LOT OF TRICYCLES
OWNED BY RETIRED PEOPLE,

BUT NONE OF THEM WORK!

I'VE JUST GOTTEN A NEW JOB:
MEDITATION.

AT LEAST IT'S BETTER THAN
SITTING AROUND DOING
NOTHING.

I FINALLY GOT AROUND TO WATCHING THAT DOCUMENTARY ON WRIST WATCHES.

IT WAS ABOUT TIME.

WHY DID THE STADIUM GET SO HOT AFTER THE GAME?

BECAUSE ALL THE FANS LEFT.

I NEVER THOUGHT THAT ORTHOPEDIC SHOES WOULD WORK FOR ME, BUT TODAY I STAND CORRECTED.

UNFORTUNATELY, MY WIFE LEFT ME BECAUSE OF MY GAMBLING AMBITION. BUT I KNOW THAT I CAN WIN HER BACK.

YOU CAN TUNE A GUITAR, BUT YOU CAN'T TUN-A FISH.

UNLESS, OF COURSE, YOU PLAY BASS.

WHAT DO YOU CALL A SAD CUP OF COFFEE?

DEPRESSO.

THE HARVEST WAS SO BAD THIS YEAR, BUT THE FARMER HAD A TON OF SICK BEETS, SO HE DECIDED TO TRY A CAREER IN MUSIC.

AFTER SOME MINUTES, THE DETECTIVES KNEW WHAT THE MURDER WEAPON WAS.

IT WAS A BRIEF CASE.

WHAT DO YOU CALL A CUTE DOOR?

ADOPTABLE.

WHOEVER STOLE MY COPY OF MICROSOFT OFFICE, I WILL FIND YOU.

YOU HAVE MY WORD!

WHAT VEGETABLE IS SORT OF
COOL BUT NOT THAT COOL?

RADISH

I ONCE GOT A JOB IN A SHOE
RECYCLING SHOP.

MY SOLE ALMOST GOT
DESTROYED!

MY BOSS TOLD ME TO ENJOY MY DAY, SO I WENT HOME!

THE SAD NEWS IS THAT I BROKE UP WITH MY GIRLFRIEND LORRAINE BECAUSE I STARTED SEEING ANOTHER GIRL, CLAIR LEE. THE GOOD NEWS IS THAT NOW THAT LORRAINE IS GONE, I CAN NOW SEE CLAIR LEE

I ONCE THOUGHT ABOUT GOING ON
AN ALL-ALMOND DIET...

BUT THAT'S JUST NUTS!

WHY DIDN'T THE SPIDER GO TO
SCHOOL?

BECAUSE HE LEARNED
EVERYTHING ON THE WEB.

MY WIFE BEGGED ME TO STOP MAKING POLICE-RELATED PUNS, SO I TOLD HER THAT I WOULD GIVE IT ARREST.

SOMEONE TOTE OFF THE FIFTH MONTH FROM MY CALENDAR. I'M COMPLETELY DISMAYED.

I ONCE TOLD MY GIRLFRIEND THAT HER EYEBROWS WERE DRAWN TOO HIGH.

SHE SEEMED SURPRISED!

MY DAD HAS BEEN THREATENING TO SEND ME OUT IF I DON'T STOP MAKING SOUTH AMERICAN PUNS.

I'M NOT READY TO STOP, SO ALPACA MY BAGS.

AFTER A VOWEL SAVES ANOTHER VOWEL'S LIFE. THE OTHER VOWEL SAYS:

"AYE E! I OWE YOU!"

IT'S BEEN SEVERAL MONTHS SINCE I ORDERED THE BOOK "HOW TO SCAM PEOPLE ONLINE."

THE BOOK STILL HASN'T ARRIVED.

I GOT TWO WATCH DOGS,
AND I NAMED THEM

ROLEX AND TIMEX!

WHAT IS A JEHOVAH'S WITNESS'
FAVORITE BAND?

THE DOORS.

IF YOU SEE A ROBBERY AT AN APPLE STORE, DOES THAT MAKE YOU AN

IWITNESS?

WHAT DO FISH SING DURING THE HOLIDAYS IN DECEMBER?

CHRISTMAS CORALS

HOW DO SNOWMEN GET AROUND?

THEY RIDE ON ICICLES.

DID YOU HEAR ABOUT THE ITALIAN CHEF WHO DIED?

HE PASTA WAY!

WHAT'S YOUR FIRST WISH?

I WISH I WAS RICH

OKAY, THEN WHAT'S YOUR SECOND WISH, RICH?

JUST A SHORT LINE SEPARATES THE NUMERATOR FROM THE DENOMINATOR, BUT ONLY A FRACTION OF PEOPLE UNDERSTAND THIS!

I TOLD MY CAT THAT I WILL TEACH HIM HOW TO SPEAK ENGLISH

HE LOOKED AT ME AND SAID: ME? HOW?

I DON'T REALLY ENJOY PLAYING SOCCER;

I'M JUST DOING IT FOR KICKS!

MY GIRLFRIEND BORROWED $200 FROM ME. THREE YEARS AFTER WE SEPARATED, SHE RETURNED TO ME $200 EXACTLY.

I LOST INTEREST TOTALLY IN THAT RELATIONSHIP.

I LOST INTEREST TOTALLY IN THAT RELATIONSHIP.

DOES THAT MAKE IT PLAGIARISM?

MY FRIEND TONY ASKED ME NOT TO SAY HIS NAME BACKWARD, BUT I SAID Y NOT?

MY FRIENDS AND I STARTED A BAND, AND WE CALLED IT BOOKS. SO THAT NO ONE CAN JUDGE US BY OUR COVERS.

IF APPLE MADE A CAR, WHAT WOULD IT BE MISSING?

WINDOWS

WHERE IN THE BIBLE WAS IT STATES THAT MEN SHOULD MAKE THE COFFEE?

HE-BREWS

IF JESUS WERE ON EARTH TODAY, WHAT CAR WOULD HE DRIVE?

A CHRISTLER

WHAT DO YOU CALL A NERVOUS JAVELIN THROWER?

SHAKESPEARE

I JUST SAW A GUY WHOSE TOE IS MADE OF RUBBER; GUESS WHAT HIS NAME IS?

ROBERTO!

INTERVIEWER: WHY SHOULD WE HIRE YOU AS A WAITRESS?

WAITRESS: FOR STARTERS, I BRING A LOT TO THE TABLE, SIR.

YESTERDAY I ACCIDENTALLY DROPPED MY PILLOW ON THE FLOOR.

IT LOOKS LIKE IT NOW HAS A CONCUSHION.

WHY DID JEFF BEZOS GET DIVORCED?

HE NEEDED MORE SPACE

GUESS WHAT? SOMEONE COMPLIMENTED MY PARKING TODAY! THEY LEFT A SWEET NOTE ON MY WINDSHIELD THAT SAID, "PARKING FINE."

HOW MUCH DOES A RAINBOW WEIGH?

NIT MUCH, THEY'RE PRETTY LIGHT

A LOT OF PEOPLE CAN'T DISTINGUISH BETWEEN ETYMOLOGY AND ENTOMOLOGY. THEY BUG ME IN WAYS I CAN'T PUT INTO WORDS.

WHAT'S THE BEST DAY TO COOK?

FRY-DAY

I'M NOT SAYING THAT I'M ATTRACTIVE, BUT WHEN I TAKE OFF MY CLOTHES IN THE BATHROOM, I TURN THE SHOWER ON.

I DON'T TRUST EDAM CHEESE;

I FEEL LIKE IT IS MADE BACKWARDS.

I THINK MY WIFE HAS CHANGED; SHE NOW APOLOGIZES. TODAY SHE SAID SHE WAS SORRY FOR EVER MARRYING ME.

WHAT DID THE CARPENTER SAY WHEN HE FINISHED BUILDING HIS HOUSE?

I NAILED IT!

I IOST THREE FINGERS ON MY RIGHT HAND, SO I ASKED THE DOCTOR IF I WOULD STILL BE ABLE TO WRITE WITH IT. L HE RESPONDED,

"YES, BUT I WOULDN'T COUNT ON IT."

WHAT KIND OF PLANTS GO OR GROW IN THE TOILET?

TOILET TREES

TEACHER: JOHN, TELL ME WHAT OBLIVIOUS MEANS

JOHN: I HAVE NO IDEA

WHAT'S THE BEST DAY TO SIT?

SAT-URDAY

TODAY, I STARTED AN ARGUMENT WITH MY WIFE IN AN ELEVATOR;

I WAS WRONG ON SO MANY LEVELS.

MY 6-YEAR-OLD DAUGHTER LINED UP ALL HER DOLLS TOWARDS THE OUTER GRILL.

IT LOOKS LIKE SHE'S MAKING A BARBIE QUEUE.

YESTERDAY I ATE A CLOCK; IT WAS VERY TIME-CONSUMING, ESPECIALLY WHEN I GO BACK FOR SECONDS.

I TRIED DONATING BLOOD TODAY, BUT I WILL NOT TRY THIS EVER AGAIN. THERE WERE TOO MANY QUESTIONS BEING ASKED "WHOSE BLOOD IS IT?" "WHY IS IT IN A BUCKET?" "WHERE DID YOU GET IT FROM?"

IF MONEY DOESN'T GROW ON TREES, THEN WHY DO BANKS HAVE BRANCHES?

MY TEACHERS TOLD ME I'D NEVER AMOUNT TO MUCH SINCE I PROCRASTINATE SO MUCH.

I TOLD THEM, "JUST YOU WAIT!"

BOY: DAD, I HAVE NOTHING TO DO

DAD: PLEASE DON'T DO IT HERE!

MY TEACHER THREATENED ME RECENTLY; HE SAID, "IF YOU THINK BY AN INCH AND TALK BY THE YARD, I WILL KICK YOU BY THE FOOT!"

TIME IS A DRUG, AND IT IS SO POWERFUL, YOU KNOW WHY?

BECAUSE IT IS GIVEN TO US ONLY IN SMALL DOSES.

I JUST REGISTERED IN COLLEGE. AS I WAS ABOUT TO ENTER THE CLASSROOM, I SAW A POST

"TIME WILL PASS, WILL YOU?"

WHY IS IT DANGEROUS TO TRUST THE STAIRS?

BECAUSE IT IS ALWAYS UP TO SOMETHING

WIFE: I'VE LEARNED HOW TO DEAL WITH YOU, MY HUSBAND, AND HAVE A PEACEFUL MARRIAGE

DAD: BY SIMPLY USING A LITTLE SIGH-CHOLOGY

WHAT GETS A SLAP AND A CLAP
FOR WORKING?

A MOSQUITO

WHAT GETS SKINNED EVERY
TIME IT LEAVES THE BUNCH?

BANANAS

MY WIFE TOLD ME TO PICK UP 8 CANS OF SODA ON MY WAY HOME FROM WORK...

SHE WAS PRETTY MAD WHEN I ONLY PICKED SEVEN UP.

I SEE PEOPLE SQUANDER MONEY, AND THIS IS SO HARD FOR ME TO WITNESS BECAUSE I CANNOT HELP THEM

TWO EGOISTS WERE
DISCUSSING AND ARGUING:

IT IS A CASE OF
AN EYE FOR AN EYE.

WHEN YOU HAVE HORSE SENSE,
IT MEANS YOU HAVE STABLE
THINKING COUPLES WITH THE
ABILITY TO SAY NAY.

THREE THIEVES WERE TRYING TO ESCAPE WITH THEIR LOOT THROUGH A WINDOW. IN THE PROCESS, ONE TORE HIS LEFT FOOT "OUCH, I MAY NEED SOME STITCHES," HE SAID. THE OTHER RESPONDED, "A STITCH IN TIME SAVES CRIME.

IF YOU USE YOUR FRIENDS TOO MUCH, THEY WON' LAST.

WHAT DOES BRO STEVE DO? HIS TROUBLES ARE ALWAYS BEHIND HIM.

HE IS A SCHOOL BUS DRIVER.

WHEN IT COMES TO GIVING, SOME PEOPLE WILL STOP ANYTHING.

MY HUSBAND IS OFTEN
GENEROUS TO A FAULT,

IF THE FAULT IS HIS OWN.

JOHN'S DAD HAS BEEN LEFT
ALONE BECAUSE HE IS ALWAYS
ASKING FOR A LOAN

I GOT ARRESTED FOR
IMPERSONATING A POLITICIAN.

I DIDN'T DO MUCH; I JUST SAT
AROUND DOING NOTHING.

JMANAGING YOUR EARNINGS
REQUIRES A BUDGET

A BUDGET IS AN ATTEMPT TO
LIVE BELOW YOUR YEARNINGS.

DAD: YOUR BROTHER'S DREAMS COULDN'T COME THROUGH. DO YOU KNOW WHY?
HE SLEPT TOO MUCH.

THE PROPRIETOR HAD THE RIGHT TO LOCK UP THE CLASSROOM, BUT HE WASN'T RIGHT TO DO IT.

MY HOTEL TRIED TO CHARGE ME TEN DOLLARS EXTRA FOR AIR CONDITIONING.

THAT WASN'T COOL.

A HONEY BREAD WALKS INTO A BAR AND ORDERS A BEER. THE BARTENDER SAYS,

"SORRY, WE DON'T SERVE FOOD HERE."

WHAT DID THE OCEAN SAY TO THE BEACH?

NOTHING, IT JUST WAVED.

I HATE IT WHEN PEOPLE SAY AGE IS ONLY A NUMBER.

AGE IS NOT A NUMBER; IT IS CLEARLY A WORD!

AN APPLE A DAY KEEPS THE DOCTOR AWAY.

THAT IS, IF YOU THROW IT HARD ENOUGH.

I ASKED MY NEW DATE TO MEET ME AT THE GYM, BUT SHE NEVER SHOWED UP. I'M NOT DISAPPOINTED; I GUESS THIS JUST MEANS THAT THE TWO OF US AREN'T GOING TO WORK OUT.

DID YOU HEAR ABOUT THE ATM THAT GOT ADDICTED TO MONEY?

IT SUFFERED FROM WITHDRAWALS AND BALANCE CHECKS.

A SLICE OF APPLE PIE IS $1.50 IN JAMAICA AND $2.00 IN THE BAHAMAS. THESE ARE THE NEW PIE RATES OF THE CARIBBEAN.

MY DOCTOR TOLD ME I WAS
GOING DEAF.

THE NEWS WAS DIFFICULT FOR
ME TO HEAR.

WHICH DAYS ARE THE WEAKEST?
THAT WILL BE MONDAYS,
TUESDAYS, WEDNESDAYS,
THURSDAYS, AND FRIDAYS; THEY
ARE WEEKDAYS.

I THINK ONE OF MY CHILDREN HAS BEEN PUTTING GLUE ON MY ANTIQUE WEAPONS COLLECTION. THEY ALL DENY IT, BUT I'M STICKING TO MY GUNS!

MY ENGLISH TEACHER WAS CONVICTED OF A CRIME, SADLY HE HAD TO COMPLETE THE SENTENCE

I WENT TO THE LIBRARY RECENTLY; THEN, I ASKED THE LIBRARIAN IF BOOKS ABOUT PARANOIA WERE AVAILABLE. SHE LOOKED UP AND WHISPERED, "THEY'RE RIGHT BEHIND YOU."

I JUST BOUGHT A HEN; SHE REGULARLY COUNTS HER OWN EGGS.

SHE'S A REAL MATHAMACHICKEN!

I DON'T REALLY ATTEND FUNERALS THAT START BEFORE NOON. I GUESS I'M JUST NOT A MOURNING PERSON!

WHY DO TREES APPEAR SUSPICIOUS ON SUNNY DAYS?

THEY APPEAR SUSPICIOUS BECAUSE THEY JUST SEEM A LITTLE SHADY!

WHAT DID THE POLICEMAN SAY
TO HIS BELLY BUTTON?

YOU'RE UNDER A VEST!

THE MATH BOOK ALWAYS LOOKS
SO SAD; WHY?

BECAUSE OF ALL OF ITS WORD
PROBLEMS!

I ASKED A QUESTION FROM MY DAD, AND HE COULDN'T ANSWER. I ASKED, "IF TWO VEGANS GET IN A FIGHT, IS IT STILL REGARDED AS BEEF?

I HARDLY BUY PRE-SHREDDED CHEESE. BECAUSE I THINK DOING IT YOURSELF IS GRATE.

I HAVE A GREAT JOKE ABOUT COVID.

BUT I'D RATHER NOT SPREAD IT.

I JUST SAW A GROUP OF SCHOLARS EATING; THEY SAID THEY WERE HUNGRY. DO YOU KNOW WHAT THEY WERE EATING?

ACADEMIA NUTS.

DID YOU HEAR THE RUMOR ABOUT BUTTER?

YES, I DID, BUT I'M NOT GOING TO SPREAD IT!

WHY DID THE OLD MAN FALL INTO THE WELL?

BECAUSE HE COULDN'T SEE WELL!

WHAT DO YOU CALL A FACTORY
THAT SELLS GREAT PRODUCTS?

A SATISFACTORY!

WHY WAS THE MAN STOOPING IN
FRONT OF THE STATION?

HE SAW THE STOP SIGN AND GOT
TIRED.

WHY DID THE INVISIBLE MAN
TURN DOWN THE JOB OFFER?

HE COULDN'T SEE HIMSELF
DOING IT!

WANT TO SEE A DOCUMENTARY I
MADE ABOUT CONSTRUCTION?

I'M STILL WORKING ON IT!

I WAS REALLY ANGRY AT MY FRIEND MARK FOR STEALING MY DICTIONARY. I TOLD HIM:

"I WILL DEAL WITH YOU, MARK, MY WORDS!"

THERE'S A NEW DATING SERVICE IN PRAGUE.

IT'S CALLED CZECH-MATE.

I WAS JUST REMINISCING ABOUT THE BEAUTIFUL HERB GARDEN I HAD WHEN I WAS GROWING UP.

GOOD THYMES.

WHAT DID STEPHEN CURRY SAY ABOUT THE SURPRISE MEAL?

HE SAID IT CONTAINED CURRY.

DID YOU HEAR ABOUT THE VEGETABLE WORKING OUT?

THE DUDE IS SHREDDED

WHO IS THE MOST LONELY OF ALL THE RICHEST MEN IN THE WORLD?

ALONE MUSK.

SADLY, MY WIFE AND I LET
ASTROLOGY GET BETWEEN US.
IT TAURUS APART.

I ONCE GOT FIRED FROM A
CANNED JUICE FACTORY.
APPARENTLY, I JUST COULDN'T
CONCENTRATE.

WHAT DO YOU CALL BILL GATES
WHEN HE'S FLYING?

A BILL-IN-AIR.

PEOPLE SPEAK A DIFFERENT
LANGUAGE WHEN THEY GET TO
THE MIDDLE OF THE EARTH. IT IS
CALLED CORE-EAN

WHY ARE BAKERS SO RICH?

THEY MAKE SO MUCH DOUGH.

WHAT DO WE CALL A CRIMINAL LANDING AN AIRPLANE?

CONDESCENDING.

MY SON GOT ANGRY AT ME TODAY. I TOLD HIM, "SKY'S THE LIMIT FOR YOU."

HE WANTS TO BE AN ASTRONAUT.

THIS TIME TEN YEARS AGO, I ASKED MY LOVER, BEST FRIEND, CHILDHOOD SWEETHEART, AND THE ONE MY HEART BEATS FOR TO MARRY ME, AND THEY ALL SAID NO.

I THINK MY WIFE STILL FINDS ME SEXY AFTER ALL THESE YEARS. ANYTIME I WALK PAST HER, SHE SAYS,

"WHAT AN ASS!"

IT TAKES GUTS FOR YOU TO DONATE ANY OF YOUR ORGANS.

BY THE TIME I FOUND OUT THAT MY TOASTER WASN'T WATER PROOFED, I WAS SHOCKED.

I RECEIVED A TEXT FROM MY WIFE SAYING, "IT'S OVER BETWEEN US" I WAS SO RELIEVED WHEN SHE TEXTED ME AGAIN AFTER A FEW MINUTES, SAYING, "SORRY, WRONG NUMBER."

MY GIRLFRIEND ALWAYS GETS MAD EACH TIME I TAMPER WITH HER RED WINE. RECENTLY I ADDED LEMONADE AND ORANGE JUICE. NOW SHE'S SANGRIA THAN EVER.

SOMEONE SHOULD PLEASE CREATE A DRINK AND NAME IT "OCCASIONALLY" SO THAT WHEN ASKED IF I DRINK, I CAN ALWAYS SAY, "I ONLY DRINK OCCASIONALLY."

THE PERSON THAT STOLE MY PLACE IN THE QUEUE, YOU CAN'T GO SCOT-FREE; I'M AFTER YOU NOW.

I BOUGHT A DOG FROM A BLACKSMITH TODAY; AS I TOOK HIM INTO THE HOUSE, HE MADE A BOLT FOR THE DOOR

MY BOSS NOTICED THAT I ALWAYS FALL SICK ON WEEKDAYS. HE ASKED WHY AND I TOLD HIM IT WAS MY WEEKEND IMMUNE SYSTEM.

EACH TIME I'M BOTHERED ABOUT SOMETHING, MY FRIEND KEEPS ASKING ME TO CHEER UP. HE SAYS, "IT COULD BE WORSE; YOU COULD BE STUCK UNDERGROUND IN A HOLE FULL OF WATER." I KNOW HE MEANS WELL.

TODAY I SAW SOMEONE WAVING. I WASN'T SURE IF THEY WERE WAVING AT ME OR WAVING AT SOMEONE BEHIND ME. IN SHORT, I LOST MY LIFEGUARD JOB TODAY.

I WAS DRIVING TO THE AIRPORT IN MY CAR. I GOT TO A PLACE AND SAW A SIGN "AIRPORT LEFT." I IMMEDIATELY TURNED MY CAR AROUND AND RETURNED HOME.

JUST SO THAT EVERYONE IS CLEAR, I'M GOING TO PUT ON MY GLASSES.

MY WIFE PHONED ME TO TELL ME THAT THREE LADIES IN HER WORKPLACE HAD JUST RECEIVED A BOUQUET OF FLOWERS AND THEY WERE ALL GORGEOUS. I TOLD HER THAT'S PROBABLY WHY.

TIME MAY HEAL EVERY, BUT NOT WHEN YOU'RE SITTING IT OUT IN A DOCTOR'S WAITING ROOM.

MY DAD ASKED MY FRIEND SAM TO SING A SONG ABOUT THE IPHONE, AND THEN SAMSUNG

MY ENGLISH TEACHER WAS CRYING. I TRIED TO CONSOLE HIM BY PATTING HIS BACK AND SAYING "THERE," "THEIR," "THEY'RE."

MY BEST FRIEND CALLED ME FROM PRISON. HE SAID, "YOU KNOW HOW WE FINISH EACH OTHER'S SENTENCES?"

I ASKED MY WIFE TODAY IF I WAS THE ONLY ONE SHE HAD BEEN WITH, AND SHE SAID YES; OTHERS HAVE BEEN NINES AND TENS.

A DRUG DEALER SOLD A PAIR OF SHOES TO ME, I DON'T KNOW WHAT HE LACED IT WITH, BUT IT GOT ME TRIPPING ALL DAY LONG.

I WAS HAVING CHALLENGES WITH THE INTERNET ON THE FARM. SO I MOVED THE COMPUTER AND MODEM TO THE BARN, AND NOW I HAVE A STABLE CONNECTION.

SOMEONE MADE A TYPO ON MY GRANDAD'S TOMB. IT WAS A GRAVE MISTAKE.

DO NOT BLAME ANYONE ELSE ON THE ROAD YOU ARE ON. THIS IS YOUR OWN ASPHALT!

I SENT MY HEARING AIDS FOR REPAIRS TWO WEEKS AGO, AND I HAVEN'T HEARD ANYTHING SINCE.

DO YOU KNOW THE LAST THING MY GRANDFATHER SAID TO ME BEFORE HE DIED?
"GRANDSON, WATCH HOW FAR I CAN KICK THIS BUCKET."

ABOUT TEN DECADES AGO, EVERYONE RODE HORSES, AND ONLY THE RICH COULD AFFORD CARS. BUT TODAY, EVERYONE RIDES CARS, AND ONLY THE RICH CAN AFFORD HORSES. SEE HOW THE STABLES HAVE TURNED

THERAPIST: IT SEEMS LIKE YOU HAVE AN ACUTE PHOBIA FOR MARRIAGE. DO YOU RECOGNIZE THE SYMPTOMS?
MAN: I CAN'T SAY I DO
THERAPIST: EXACTLY, THAT'S ONE OF THE SYMPTOMS.

DAD JOKES

Loading...

Made in the USA
Columbia, SC
15 June 2022

61773171R00057